The Gay Lie

The End of "Homosexual" Discrimination

David O'Brien

ISBN: 978-1-960245-16-8

This book can free anyone from the pain of "homosexual" discrimination.

DEDICATION

To those in the night of the city.
I stand to give you Light.

CONTENTS

DON'T READ THIS…

…unless you want to encounter truth spoken in love.

Mockers are, sadly, worse off than fools.

A fool repeats the same mistake over and over, in a loop, because of some mistake in reasoning. That error can be fixed. The gap can be closed, which will then change the lifestyle pattern.

There is also hope for mockers—great hope, but they'll have to lay down their mask.

There is a pot of gold at the end of the journey I'll lead you down. Healing for your heart. Rest for your head.

Prepare yourself to take this journey. You will find a cool, refreshing stream within the words of these pages.

Chapter 1
The Gay Lie

What does "gay" mean?

The word originated from the French "gai" in the 12th century, with the meaning of "joyful" or "merry." It evolved some but later became a label—a cover actually—used to hide some things.

For all of human history, the most desirable and beautiful thing to ever behold is a bride adorned in her wedding dress. The natural desire for such glory has caused men to lay down their lives to obtain it.

The word gay could describe the bride on that day, swept off her feet by a worthy groom. Or it could easily describe the groom, on the truly gayest day of his life, the happiest day, the day he took his wife home with him.

Is it possible to live a lie? We've all been lied to. That's unavoidable. But to build one's life on a lie is like building on a foundation that's not level or that's cracked. You can do it, but something will always be off balance. Could it be that you have been building on a lie? On "the gay lie"?

In the 17th and 18th centuries, "gay" was eventually used to label *opposite-sex*, "promiscuous" or "hedonistic" lifestyles. That was part of "the gay lie," a band-aide slapped on people whose lives had become derailed

Promiscuous means "having or characterized by many temporary sexual relationships." Hedonism is a philosophy that puts pleasure, of any kind, above everything else as the ultimate good and goal in life. It seems right in some way, but it *always* ends in pain.

The word they chose to describe themselves meant "happy," but were they? Having to use alcohol, late nights and temporary partners for pleasure—was that really gay? Or could the opposite have been true? Could it be that they were hooked, that they had to artificially add pleasure *because they weren't happy*? They lived a pendulum swing. They went from depression, wondering if they were "ok" and not liking what they saw in the mirror, to running after quick and physical pleasure again. And the cycle continued, with pain, over and over.

In the mid-20th century, the label was adopted by those who had or acted on sexual attraction to people of their same sex. This was new. But again, was it true for them, or was there another reason they started using it? Could it have been a cover? Does "happy" describe same sex-attraction?

Could it be that to acknowledge same-sex experiences and/or attraction was too painful? Could it be that it would bring too much pain from those who would look down on or judge? Yes.

Was it true? Does being sexually attracted to one's own sex make happiness in life reach the top of the scale? Or was the word again being used as a cover? Could it be that "gay" didn't describe either of these two groups that used it?

Using this cover masks a problem; it says, "Nothing wrong here—we're all just happy. We're extra happy." That can be a thick bandage over a painful and terrible looking wound. The desire to hide such a wound could be sooo strong that this bandage was hard to take off.

Chapter 2
Healed from Shame

Shame has a paralyzing effect. It can bind a person, and that tight bondage can be so hard to try to wriggle out of! It can feel suffocating!! But one can cut through and come out of it.

Shame makes a person recoil and hide from being seen. It also sends out poisonous arrows from the inner being of the one who has it. They shoot out through the mouth and hit vulnerable areas of people nearby.

Shame started long ago in Eden's Garden and had nothing to do with sexuality. Adam and Eve had been "naked and unashamed" before then. Covered in God's own glory at all times, it's like they were painted gold and shining. Once they left God's splendorous light, they shrunk down into shame and hiding, rather than standing bold and upright. And when God asked Adam what he had done, he did something his counterpart probably didn't expect. He shot her with an arrow from his mouth, of accusation.

Since then, we've all experienced and acted on shame at times and in various areas. Shame makes uncomfortable on the inside. It causes people to *accuse* others, to overly blame, to judge down on others, in order to alleviate shame's inner pressure.

So how does this relate to what we're talking about, "the gay lie"? The bandage that people hid under—"nothing to see here, folks; we're all really happy"—was because of pain from *accusations* launched against them by people who couldn't understand or relate to them, and who had shame.

Many westerners today don't know what the word, "fornication" means (even though they use its abbreviation constantly). It's a deviation from God's plan of covenant-sexuality. In other words, God created the covenant of "union for life" (or "marriage"), to exclusively house sexuality. He requires people to commit for life to each other, in order to enjoy intimacy with each other. This is his designed way. All nations of the earth at one time knew this and prohibited "fornication" (i.e., sex without the ultimate commitment).

But the Western countries of the world had major cultural shifts that created an avalanche of fornication. As this lifestyle was against God's created order, it caused shame in people. That shame caused accusation to shoot out from them—into unsuspecting bystanders around them.

Shame is an unnatural fear of being seen. The Western countries were herded downhill, headlong into fornication, bringing heavy shame. This was done by misinformation. They even removed the word, "fornication" from the culture, including from the Bible. The word was too painful for society to face, so *they blanked it out.*

So what does this have to do with "the gay lie"? Let me tell you: it was the opposite-sex-attracted, fornicating people that sent the accusations against those with any same-sex attraction. Their judgment came down swift and hard, on anyone with the slight appearance or possibility of same sex attraction. Why? Their own shame! They wanted a scapegoat, someone they felt they could blame to alleviate their own inner shame.

They launched the accusations, to feel better about how they look in the mirror for a moment. They shot the dart of homo-sexuality out of their mouths at people around them. It hit people and held them like a giant spider web.

Who was the victim? The one being accused!!!

It's no wonder that those who were accused utilized "the gay lie"! They had to keep their heads down, hiding as in a bunker from incoming showers of accusation.

Most people who come under the heavy microscope of those who accuse, succumb to its pressure. They are crushed under it, and stay there under the weight of it.

Many who cover themselves with the gay lie have been abused by powerful, accusation-filled words of shame. It seems like a weight too hard to get out from under. However, the Light of truth can pierce through and rescue anyone under any heap of any lies.

An outsider may asume that those who take refuge in a community would be safe there. But shame seeps out when people are pressed down, and a spear can come from someone closest to a person. The tongue can bring out the stench of an atmosphere that's been polluted by the abuse of sexuality.

Someone said, "God is always on the side of the oppressed." I believe that.

Why did Jesus hang around prostitutes and those rejected by society? For one, he was more at home among them, being largely rejected himself. For two, he saw the treasures in them! He saw their value, which is never diminished, despite outward treatment. He sees YOU this way, with powerful eyes, even if from afar.

You're like a coin of incalculable value, and despite any outward experience, mistreatment or damage, your value has never dropped.

You are not the sum of what any human has said, thought or whispered about you. Step out of that box.

Hearing many accusations may have made you very strong—very tough, and calloused. They may make you strive harder to "act like a man," as if standing up to an invisible oppressor, someone from the past who set a standard too high. Well, their standard is unattainable; it was a bar set too high because of their own shame. It was set out of reach! It was a lie passed down through them. And you can bounce back and defeat any lie!

Lately in the West, opposite-sex attracted people, who engage in fornication, have lessened their accusative, missile-launching against same-sex attracted people. The simple reason is that the numbers and influence of same-sex attracted people increased. People respond to numbers, power and influence!

There is another major source of the gay lie: *heavily religious Christians.* They carry a religious atmosphere that often invokes terror on the common people of the world. When they come around, it's like America's Wild West, people close their windows, lock their doors and stay inside.

Why?

Many Christians have not been able to handle the increased sexual temptations of the current Western culture. But instead of humbly acknowledging their own issue, they've often *covered it up* with a hypocritical mask. That mask can be the most fierce, scary mask out there, as it's used while blasting people who are hiding behind a shield for dear life.

Blasting people doesn't make the one who does it more innocent, but it does divert attention and keep him or her hidden.

This has probably contributed to the gay lie the most: the religious people, the ladies who seem so "good," dressed in their Sunday best, but how they see themselves in their personal mirror of reflection is very different.

That façade and constant, painful, grinding pressure was too much on people's backs. If people feel they can never escape their past, under the brutal inspection of perfectionism, it's easier to embrace it as an identity.

How did Jesus treat the people of his day? He treated each one with dignity! With a kind of rare love, previously unknown to mankind. How did he treat the overt "sinners" and criminals? He spent his time with them. He wiped their tears.

How do his self-proclaimed followers treat the *same* people? Sometimes with disdain, alienation and hypocritical judging—hypocritical because they have problems in the same category that they accuse.

Jesus looked at each person and each case differently, diagnosed them as a compassionate physician, and used supernatural power to heal them freely. This is very different than hypocrisy. It is the opposite, really. And he did this for *everyone* who got around him and allowed it, no exception.

The good news is that this is the way God sees you and me. In his kingdom—*his* country, his territory—his children are all diverse and united spiritually, with no outward discrimination.

Jesus came to the hostile environment of Earth. Why? To stand between you and the rock of judgment people want to throw at you, and to take the rock for you, in the face. He also came to bring healing to the chasm, to bring new life, and to bring about a new way on earth. He revealed the way of God's Country of Love.

Jesus came to bring a new start, a new innocence, supernaturally. He didn't come down on people who had given their innocence up, nor did he see their case as outside of his jurisdiction and ability to fix. He healed them, untwisting their insides in whatever way they needed.

That same power he used is available today. Without it, I couldn't be writing this book! *I myself received it.* And I can give it to anyone around me who needs it.

People don't need power to reach a religious standard. Perfection does not exist in humanity. But if anyone has been disfigured by shame, we can reverse that supernaturally—*no problem.* And I can give you a different image of you than you have seen. It is the way God sees you, absolutely glorious. As you see it, you will be able to supernaturally adjust to it, and display yourself, as he has made you, at your finest.

Chapter 3

The Devastation of Ab-use

God only creates amazing things. Even the "ordinary" of his creation is shown to be absolutely amazing. But there are some things that we as observers call exquisite: for example, a uniquely purple flower. And some people undervalue such beauty.

Some have no category for uniqueness. Being narrow minded, they reject it. Others feel threatened by it, so they try to ignore it, downplay and suppress it, or reject it. Others try to possess it for themselves. Some would trample on it. Some would publicly mock and attack it.

When an exquisite flower is stepped on, it cannot defend itself. It is unable to stand up to the force and weight of a descending boot. Inevitably, the flower is crushed. Its form is changed. It is misshapen, altered, perhaps, for the rest of its life.

The one who stepped on it continues on, barely noticing what he or she has done, oblivious to the value of the exquisite creation. But God has built into this flower a unique ability. When crushed, it releases its fragrance. And despite being crushed, the flower retains its original nature and its value. This analogy is the power of forgiveness.

There are many forms of abuse that go on in the world. One of the worst is physical, *sexual-related* abuse.

I talked about verbal abuse in the last chapter—putting people in a box by poisonous, accusative words, especially related to *identity*. Those words, like a rope put on an elephant's leg from its youth, can be used to alter a person's whole future.

All abuse is the crossing of a boundary. It's like breaking and entering, and then leaving footprints on a person's nice, hardwood floors.

Each person was created with boundaries. The job of parents and other adults is to protect those boundaries and ensure they stay intact while the child grows. They are to protect their psyche—their inner mirror image—and the way they see others in life.

Some cultures call these "inalienable" rights, given by God. Regardless, in every culture, one way or another, individual boundaries are recognized. How people treat others' boundaries constitutes morality. So what is "sexual abuse"?

Abuse literally means, "Ab-normal use." This includes the use of a thing in a way that it was not designed. For example, to open a door with a knife is to abuse the doorknob, and the knife—they weren't meant to be used that way. A key is to be used in a doorknob to open it. And both the key and the doorknob are happy. There's no damage.

Why do people abuse? The reason is selfishness, because there's pleasure involved. At the heart of it may be ignorance or deception. And usually, the one who does it was abused himself or herself.

To understand "abnormal use," we need to understand *the purpose* of sexuality. The uniting of the male and female sex organs has the potential to produce new life. Without it, no one on earth would be here. It is *the way* to reproduce. But that's definitely not all.

The brain is involved in a unique way in sexuality. The body goes through sophisticated changes while growing into adulthood that allow for this. (Note: normal sexuality is for adults only).

The male and female organs fit together perfectly like a key in a lock When united, there are many chain reactions that take place in the body, in the brain and the eyes. They allow for a time of intimate *bonding*, that involves great pleasure. This is the highest natural form of physical pleasure, released in the pleasure center of the brain, and it bonds the two people together.

In other words, normal sexuality is for reproduction and for bonding—for *unity*, to enhance a relationship between two people who are very, very different. There are only two sex organs—the male and the female ones. Other parts of the body, like a woman's breasts, change during that time of private intimacy. But the sex organs are unique.

Sexuality is designed to enhance a lifelong bond that people have mutually consented to. This bond also benefits the kids that can result from the act. It is a reward for the commitment, a unifier of the relationship, and an incentive to continue on in it.

Normal sex is *for* the fully committed relationship, for pleasure, and for kids. And it is private. The covenant, called "marriage," has been found in every country and culture in the world from the beginning. Why? Because it didn't start as an invention of mankind; it was part of the design of the Creator.

When abused, sex can go from being a blessing to a point of regret. It still has the major impact in the brain that it would've had if it were in the covenant. But without the covenant connection, it's like a severed, live, electrical wire, moving like a snake in the street. It's *dangerous*. One of the best things a person can do for another is to protect his or her boundaries. One of the worst things is to abuse them or allow them to be abused.

In traditional Hawaiian culture, a married woman wears a flower over her left ear as a beautiful sign of being already part of a married union and unavailable. Virgins also traditionally wear one, over the right ear. This was for order and celebration of a good thing, also to signify availability for a lifelong relationship. Sexuality being reserved for the boundaries of marriage, a man who saw the flower over the right ear knew the woman was potentially available to attempt to court. There was no guarantee of a relationship.

Contrast this with seduction. In an abusive situation, a woman will seek to coercively over-attract, *hook* and catch a man—sometimes for survival. The end of it for both parties is pain. In fact, the greater the pleasure of that temporary encounter, the more pain the man will have because the deeper the hook is set in his brain. This is a bondage. It's not marriage. It traps and hauls a man away. It is ab-use. The woman in this situation is in a prison of her own, from previous abuse.

Men were designed to be protectors, humble gentlemen, and mass liberating warriors, but if they take the bait of this hook, they end up hauled off in an internal prison. This is the result of sex ab-use.

Sex is very, very valuable. It's like a diamond meant to be placed under a secure, unbreakable glass, with maximum security guarding it. Everything of value must be guarded.

Sex was designed as a bonding reward. Commitment carries reward. Full commitment is noble. It involves both risk and reward. It is of character. When someone commits to love, serve, protect, respect...*for life*—it's not just any commitment, but a covenant. It is rewarded with God's permission of intimacy. The boundary is removed, the wedding veil lifted. The woman can be known fully by the man and vice versa.

Now sexuality is introduced, on the foundation of that mutual, true commitment. Part of its design is the first time—designed to be the most impactful. It's "the cherry on top" of the life-long commitment. It's an exquisite, shared experience unlike any other, for a lifelong memory, for bonding. That is its purpose.

Sex is ab-used when it's not reserved for that full-commitment relationship, but done beforehand. The flower is trampled on and left. When that happens, the benefit of the first time of that amazing union is missed completely.

The ab-use of sex always results in the abuse of people and oneself. People being abused sexually is *extremely* common in the Western world today. When it happens before reaching adulthood, a snapshot of that event is taken. Throughout one's life, that snapshot may attempt to take a person's mind back to that event. For them, the impact of the first time can have a *negative* effect. They are dragged back, by that image, causing a repeat of the same type of abuse. Until a greater force removes that power!

A person can be frozen in time, back at the event of that boundary being breached. Their growth and development can stop there in some ways. Something enters their life at that moment, and goes forward with them, to dictate their thoughts and desires. What came out of that experience may replay the rest of their lives—*unless addressed and healed.*

So, as you can see, the normal use of sex is bonding, pleasurable, safe, private, and priceless. It is rewarding. It is reserved for the highest quality of covenant-relationship, and is so powerful it can produce life. On the other hand, the abuse of sex is painful, and can be devastating. And the worst part is that it can change one's sense of self-worth and identity.

Chapter 4
What Remains

The abuse is an event. It has an end. It's like a house fire that burns most things in the house to ash. The house itself is still standing; you are still alive after the fire is out. But among the things burned is one's past self-image. The past self-portrait of innocence and happiness is only half visible now.

In other words, the abusive act, or series of acts, is one thing. It's like the pain of being burned with a cigar in one's soul. But the other thing is the scar left from it. That's what stays far beyond the ab-use. And the worst scar is that which affects your identity.

If I have a wrong account number for my bank account, so that I can't access millions I have there that I desperately need to be able to eat, that would be tragic! But far worse is being fed a lie that puts me in a prison too small for the real me, so that at all times the bars of it cuts through my actual being and reduces my actions.

Real identity comes *before* actions. If I'm fed a lie about my identity, that will affect my actions. But still, in reality, my actions don't make me what I am. My actions come *second*. They don't define me, no matter how much they may affect me.

If abuse is breaking and entering, the mud left on the floor of one's life afterward is the affected feelings, memory, and self-view left over.

So, what is the disfiguring of identity? It's like the burglar changing the lock on the front door, so that he can come back over and over and access the place with his own key.

"Gay" is a lie.

There are a couple things that abusing sex *is not.* First, it is not a root issue, and second, it does not create identity.

Sexuality is so powerful physically and mentally that abusing it can easily alter the brain. It can alter feelings. It can change desires. It can cause cravings. A hook in the brain, when pulled, can be just like a hook deeply impeded in a fish. It can pull a person out of his or her intended environment.

Your identity is not your sexuality, marital status, or feelings or experiences. You are greater than all of those things, which are simply characteristics. Your identity is higher.

Some people take skin color or national origin as their identity, which then becomes their basis of living: who they're around, what they are interested in, how they feel and think. One's origin and color are real, but those things didn't exist when we go way back in time, and yet people still did exist. Those people had the same nature and actual identity as you.

Some people go by male or female as an identity. That is still an attribute. It goes pretty close to identity, but even it is still not. People may say, "human." But what is a human? There are characteristics we can observe, but identity goes deeper than those things!

People are not just bodies walking around. They have an inner being. They have thoughts, emotions, etc. But even those aren't the deepest things in a person.

The life of a living thing is its spirit. When a person "breathes his last," the body is the exact same as before, just without the spirit. When a person's spirit goes out, it takes with it the reasoning and thinking and emotions, which is often called, "the soul."

You are not your body—regardless of what it's like. It's only a small part of you, and you are deeper than that. No matter *how much* abuse has happened to your body, and thereby affected your soul, it did *not* alter your spirit. You were not changed at the root-foundation level, which is the identity level.

There is help for you, for any wrong identity imprints in your soul. They can all be reversed.

We've been talking about the abuse of sexuality, of which there are many kinds. They are like mud from the spinning of a big truck tire. It gets on you, but it's only on the outside. It can be easily washed off with water.

If you want the pain and stain of an abuse or series of abuses washed off right now, do this physical act: write down what you want removed, immediately. Now touch your heart and your head. If you've done those two things, I command for you, with the Authority given to me: the mouth of the enemy be shut. And now I supernaturally patch up the deadly, horrible wound you suffered.

Chapter 5

Looking for Love…

Sexuality is unique. The ab-use of sex has the characteristics of a cliff. When a person falls off the edge of the cliff, it is very difficult to climb back up. They fall into a canyon, a rut, a place of being "stuck."

Why do people go off that cliff? Because they don't see it. Their eyes are temporarily focused slightly upward on something else as they walk off. What are people are looking for when they take that step? Oftentimes, it's love.

People's hearts have been bruised and beaten in, in multiple places. They want that internal pain alleviated. Pleasure, acceptance, and love—these are powerful motivators. But they can be used as a dangling carrot, never actually ever attained, which leads off the cliff.

Many live in a perpetual state of needing and seeking love, with repeated, painful result. It is very sad.

Love is patient. Love is kind…it does not seek its own interests first. It's not selfish. When sex-heightened pleasure in the brain is involved, selfish motives can show up easily. A drug addict can steal from his own poverty-stricken mother because the rut in his brain is seriously no joke. When the brain is hooked, the whole life can be pulled, no matter how strong a person is in other areas.

No one *intends* to go off the cliff and into the rut. This is why there's no room for judgment, but only compassion. Some are forced off of it. Others are persuaded or tricked off.

The problem with "the gay lie," which applies to all kinds of ab-use of sexuality, is that it creates a no-go zone beyond the rut. Because nothing can be questioned beyond the gay lie, nothing can be healed.

No one's nature was changed when they fell off the cliff. But because of needle-like, excessively painful, finger pointing by those secretly off a cliff themselves, the gay lie is used. It's for survival. It's like donning a gas mask in a deadly environment.

Behind that mask is a mix of all kinds of things, including innocent people being hurt over and over again. Well, I don't see or believe the gay lie. I see people—and I can go into their environment and rescue them. Because I know Love.

When you encounter Love, the finger pointing ends. Compassion flows out of love. Self-acceptance comes. You can embrace yourself. Love is non-discriminating.

Love enjoys truth, but "truth" *without* love is grinding. Love is fond of truth because the truth is really good news and liberating, for every person on earth. Truth never ends in a rut! And according to the truth, the rut is not as big a challenge as those caught in it think. It could simply be a pitstop, onto a higher, stable life full of beauty, that soars and constantly releases heavenly glory and fragrance.

True Love does not mistake the sewer for the person in it!! It has the power to shine in there, so the person sees the steps he can take, steps up and out. Love causes the person also to stay out of there, to walk beyond in life with a pep in one's step. Love embraces, regardless of where people are, as long as they let it. It won't force itself.

Truth spoken in love is powerful. Love comes first as it is the parameters that truth must stay in. When love is in place, truth spoken in it becomes medicinal. It always uplifts. It has power beyond the cliff or rut to lift people. It lifts the chin of the disappointed or discouraged, revealing that they are still glorious, unique and one-of-a-kind!

Love is not primarily human, but it can come through people. It is a super-power. Touch that is inflamed with love is power-full.

Love is attainable to all. It is not something to run off a cliff for. It is already given, but it must be discovered.

How do you get out of the canyon rut and back up over the edge of the cliff? You need something more powerful, something more attractive, something that can lift you—pure Love.

Love has nothing to do with sexuality.
Love has nothing to do with sexuality.
Love has nothing to do with sexuality.

True Love is comforting, healing, liberating, and also, at times, course-correctional. It will wait till a person can hear the truth, in order to shine healing, mending and soothing light, in order to easily fix a wounded or dysfunctional area.

Don't settle for the rut, in search of a love that doesn't exist in it. The painful counterfeit is common, and multitudes live there. But you can determine to leave it, to travel as far as it takes away from it till you find the essence of Love, which satisfies the inner being. When you have that, you'll also be able to give of it, to weary and love-thirsty souls.

Seeking love is not the only reason people go off of the cliff into the rut, of course. When someone breaches a boundary and tampers with a person's sexuality, he or she can alter the pleasure circuits of a person's brain. They activate a person's sexual desire. But that desire was designed to turn on, in the covenant, gradually.

It's like they put a chip in the brain, that is living and directs the person's desires in certain circumstances. This can also lead to the "bait and switch" scenario of the cliff and the rut. A person goes for pleasure, reaches for it, and falls off the cliff, deeper into the rut.

Some people despise the rut, but don't know how to deal with it, so they walk off of the cliff continually, each time fighting to get back up before being tricked back off again.

Others create a life over the cliff. They settle there, saying, "This is me. This is what I like. This is how I am." But their life has a lot of pain—it's brittle, too sensitive to the touch. That can be changed. It may seem like there's so little hope to get back up that cliff and learn to stay up there.

But there *is* freedom available, through a sacrifice made long ago on a torture instrument, to the death. And there is new Life available! It is possible to make it back up out of that rut!

If the rut has been a problem in the past, sex within the covenant slowly but surely adjusts the eyes to see the difference between a spouse, in the covenant, and everyone else. Boundaries are restored. And clarity comes for the journey ahead.

When you see outward rebellion, know that it's not a root. The anger in the person's heart got there somehow! If a person is saying crazy stuff, some will point a finger, but it's really a sign that they're in pain, that there's something inside that isn't resolved, same-sex abuse from the past, for example. Who wants to feel helpless and abused? It creates a rage on the inside! And no goodie two-shoe, religious-faker lady is going to put that rage out.

The problem on the inside corrupts over time. But there is a Fire that's brighter than all of this, that can reverse the corruption and change one's self view.

I said that the gay lie is a mask. By some, it is worn proudly. It gives exemption for any and everything behind it. Well, there is another, terrible abuse: when someone tries to take it off, to tell the world, "I am no longer 'gay,'" they get tortured by those still wearing that mask. They go after their past and make it super-hard for the person to get out of that box. They want that person to keep the mask on with no ability to even question it.

The whole house of cards collapses if just one person says, "I'm no longer 'gay.'" Now it's a choice. "If it's a choice, the heavy accusers' missiles will come down and we won't have a shield to hide under." So they persecute that one *mercilessly*. That's abusive. They try their best to pull them back in. Why? Love? No. Shame. Identity—a mask, a cover.

How do you beat the cliff and rut? You need help from above. You need someone standing on the cliff who can drop you a rope—some inspiration and light—and pull you up. You're going to have to be honest about your actions, and to accept and forgive yourself, despite them.

There's a logic that says, "I have done humiliating actions in secret that I am ashamed of, therefore I am ___ (something really negative) and therefore unacceptable." Listen, it's not about being worthy of Love. You are loved. That's what matters most. And any self-accusing, shameful thing you've done can be wiped away. You can be freed from its torment.

The abusive actions have to stop; certain relationships and environments must be ended and avoided. The dark power from the past must be dealt with, by a Higher Authority and power. This will end its grip on you. Also, you also need light of truth in various areas, to retrain your thinking and heal your life! Eventually, the warm Light will heal you at the deepest level, removing the roots completely.

The real thing, which is sex in the covenant as designed, will help with the rut-lifestyle and protect you from going over the cliff. Also, you will need wisdom, understanding, discretion, and various truths, to handle media programing well because there are hidden tripwires in it, no question.

If you have a religious background, you will need to learn about how religious rules fuel the fire of wrong desires and can cause a pendulum swing. Man's religion can be a dark grip, probably the deepest, dark root of the abuse of sex.

Most people in today's "technologically advanced" world are vulnerable to the rut and the cliff. But that scheme can absolutely be beat through love and truth, over time.

Chapter 6
Subjugation

What happens when someone reaches past a legitimate boundary in your life….? What happens when abused?

If the one abused gives in, in his or her heart, he or she is put in subjection under the abuser. People were designed and intended to be free. But the action of control and crossing boundaries takes a piece of that freedom from us.

Even more importantly, the person abused is brought under subjection *to the abuse.* The abuser may never be seen again. But the abuse itself can be a hard weight to get out from under. How does that work?

Because of the intricate design of sexuality, and its immense power in the brain, at the point of sexual abuse there is like a photograph snapshot taken that remains in the memory. By it, images and scenarios can influence you that wouldn't have otherwise. The brain can later be used against a person, through physical senses and that original snapshot. How do you get out of that?

The boundary that was crossed was the will. The whole abuse was intended to get a person to bow—to submit—to the abuse, to come under it. But we can win in the end! But we can soar above it all.

So the will was breached, and with the abuse came an image and feelings. After that comes shame—the feeling of guilt. The abuser will attempt to leave his or her shame *on the victim*, typically, and live as if nothing ever happened.

The abused one was not guilty!!! Even if they did bow when they could've stood, *they were the one abused!* They should have NO REMORSE and never be punished. But a sense of guilt and shame can hang around them, creating the feeling that "something is always off with me." This can lead to extra efforts to try to gain acceptance from peers, class-clowning in school, etc. There can be a despair over the question of "will anyone ever truly love me???" But nothing is actually wrong with the person! They just carry the maul marks of a bear, so to speak. It's the abuser who should be feeling guilty. That person has shame, but they hide it very well, and accuse.

The will was breached by abuse, and an image was captured that remains. Underlying shame may linger. Next is the prison. What is the prison?? A philosophy can be developed that justifies the behavior. In other words, out of self-defense, because of the shame involved, a person will change their thinking on what's acceptable or not for living. They will change their standard to fit their experience, to avoid judgment from oneself or others.

That change in philosophy and standards is a prison because it allows the abuse of sex to continue to happen. It weakens or removes a boundary, allowing more abuse. And the worst of those prisons is related to identity.

Being "a player" or "a ladies' man" or "a lover not a fighter" can be a cover for out-of-control sexuality. The gay lie is also. Get to the bottom of that and you'll find the abuse of sex.

People may say, "There's nothing wrong with a little sex!" That's a changed philosophy, and it's a cover used to smokescreen the issue. It's not about sex—without sex none of us would be here. It's about sex being used normally, within a covenant relationship, or abused outside of one.

When the philosophy is a lie, it allows for continued abuse. It makes sense that people shape a philosophy, but it doesn't help. Because on the wrong side of truth, even with a nice sounding philosophy, there is pain. And the philosophy will be used to keep the door open for more of the same abuse—including child abuse. So if someone uses the gay lie to cover a real, internal problem, the problem will never be reached and healed.

If the practice becomes an *identity*, the prison is fortified. But it's walls can still be broken through!

Chapter 7
New Shackles

Abuse is like shackles put on the wrists. They project a self-image on the person they afflict: "You are (something negative), based on the action you did or that was done to you." This lie about identity makes a person willing to comply without a fight.

You are NOT an action. OK, you did an action, and there are reasons why you did. But that did not take you down to the level of the action. If you physically trip and fall in a ditch, you don't stay where you fell and say, "This is me now. I'm here. I stay here." No, *you dust yourself off,* and you get out of the rut and back on track to where you were going.

Remember that ab-use, which is the abnormal use of sexuality and the crossing of a boundary, puts the person who gives in to it into handcuffs. Those cuffs are a new self-image, a new standard, and a new philosophy to fit their experience and feeling. The worst of these ideas is related to identity. If we swallow that pill, it goes deeper into our inner being, changing us so that we more easily accept future abuse.

It is possible to have a delayed response from the time of initial abuse to the time feelings and desires change. This is especially if the abuse happens as a child. The sexual part of the brain and body aren't developed yet, so desires won't be totally affected. But the child will still be acting and thinking somewhat differently than other kids.

What has happened is a seed has gone into the victim's heart. It may take time to grow before it sprouts into the visible world. A seed like that carries an image and a feeling, and can grow to influence a person's life. The seed of the image of the abuse of sex is like the seed of a weed. But, as with any garden, weeds can be plucked up by their roots!

One form of sex ab-use is pornography. It crosses a boundary in the mind like a bullet in the brain. Its seed, if not addressed, can become a tree with roots occupying huge amounts of kids' minds. It is born in ab-use—prostitution—and amped up by technology. It is a lie in disguise, offering immediate pleasure that dissolves into pain. A true drug that doesn't use the nostrils like cocaine, the bloodstream like heroin or the lungs like crack cocaine to affect the pleasure center of the brain. It uses the eyes.

Pornography is "THE ELEPHANT IN THE ROOM," in WHATEVER COUNTRY it's been allowed to spread. Though it has been given clearance and protection, it's *at the heart* of a multitude of abuses, crimes and consequences in today's world, affecting whole societies like a plague.

There is a road ahead for those who have fallen into any of the various abuses in the world today. The ancient saying, "Where a tree falls, there it will lay" is only true "under the sun." There is a super-natural refreshing that can lift that tree and restore it.

Light can shine down and into a person, quickly produce life, and stabilize them. Old patterns of thinking can also be replaced with new ones. Our eyes can be opened to our current state, if we are being used as a slave.

When we go outside of our own boundary, or allow someone to cross a boundary, our conscience changes. Our conscience is our inner thinking of what's acceptable. The line moves for us. If we continue, our conscience can be seared, as with a hot iron, to the point of no feeling. That's dangerous in the same way as having no feeling in one's hand. A person can touch fire and not notice it is burning the flesh off.

So to get out of the rut—to be relieved of the shackles—a person will have to loosen their mental grip, especially as far as their identity is concerned.

Chapter 8
Identity

Where does a sense of identity come from? For millennia people have been using a family name to identify themselves. It points to ancestry, which is related to ethnicity. But what about before those families began, when there were many less people? If someone surnamed "Smith" is transported back to before there were any Smiths, does that person cease to exist? No. So, family of origin is not a good foundation for identity.

Many people build their sense of identity on their profession. But that's not who or what they are. That's what they can do. Others take pride in an identity based on skin color. To someone literally colorblind, that means nothing. That is really a distinction between members of a same species. It's very shallow to put identity on race because you are more than a color on the outside of your body!

Race, height, age, weight, hair color, etc. are all *characteristics* of one's physical body, not the actual person.

Female and male are more solid distinctions. But both sexes are of one "mankind." That "all men (mankind) are created equal" refers to *value.* All were created with equal value, not equal height or athletic ability, or artistic ability, etc. Each is distinctly different, despite all being within the same human race, and all have the same value, put there by the creator. All have certain undeniable "human rights" of freedom of thought and choice, etc.

It may have been branded on your mind that you *are* just a characteristic of your body. *But you are greater.* Identity and value come not from characteristics but from origin and nature.

What is the origin of the human body, including every cell in the brain and every other part? The answer is dust and water. Our bodies are made up of minerals found in the dirt, and water. Perhaps the most common and least valuable thing on earth is dirt. Does that mean are we of no value?

Why do we have much more value than dust? The fact that we can think, feel, and use our body to do things shows *we are more than our bodies.* We have a soul (or "psyche"), with the ability to learn and feel and desire things. We also have a *spirit.*

The body is just the house, or casing, for the life. And that life is unique. Mankind rules his environment, even if poorly. He instinctively stays at the top, names and classifies all of the animals, learns and changes the earth for his own liking, etc. Why? Because the spirit of man is a ruling spirit. This makes mankind very similar to its creator and different than the other created beings.

Man was not designed to rule other people, as all have the ruling spirit. If one rules another, beyond a person's will, it is an abuse, an oppression.

Regardless of what has happened with a person's body or soul, if they are human, they were uniquely designed, uniquely gifted, made uniquely responsible, and uniquely valuable. No matter what a person does, or what has been done to them, they share this same value—because of their *nature,* which is the true, foundation of identity.

Also, each person within the human race was created with great uniqueness. Each fingerprint is different. Each person is different, and that uniqueness has value too, but it's secondary. Society celebrates an amazing musician more than an unaccomplished street sweeper, but inside is the same kind of spirit, with the same exact value.

Your sexuality is not your identity. It is partly your choice, partly a product of ancestry and genetics, partly a product of your environment. A person who has never known anything sexual, whether a child or an adult, is not a non-entity. They have an identity, and it's valuable. It is not derived from feelings, desires or actions or ideas.

Chapter 9
Religious Abuse

Many people have suffered terrible wounds from religious beatings. This religious abuse is the real reason people seek to take refuge in a box. Though it's like a cardboard box without a lid, allowing a person to still be seen, a person still will hide in it, as it seems like it's better than nothing!

I've been in countries and cultures where I've seen individuals who, by their actions or attractions, would be *boxed* and *categorized* as a different species of being if they were in the West. But in those locations, they were not! They were just people.

What does "the West" have in common? A history of religious Christianity. The liberating message called, "The Good News," in the Bible, which is for all, did not cause damage or harm to anyone. But the traditional religious posture that is not founded on that message but seeks all the time to be "good" through traditional and moral laws—that influence caused a big problem. That is what caused people to cover their weaknesses knowing there would surely be heavy weaponry aimed at them to shoot relentlessly.

The gay lie, of the 17th and 18th centuries, was no doubt because of the religious high-judges of the day.

What is a hypocrite? The word comes from the ancient Greek language. It was a compound word made up of "under" and "judge," and it was used to refer to mask-wearing actors in the theater. It meant "to judge from under a mask." This is one of the words Jesus himself used a lot, to describe the ultra-religious people of his day.

A hypocrite is someone who pretends to be innocent, and accuses/judges others. His judging is a covering for the shame that he's hiding. When there's a steady stream of almost subconscious criticizing and judging coming out of a person, it's typically because of an out-of-control area of their own life that is hidden. *They first judge themselves* internally, which is why they cling to the mask, and then they judge others.

The pointed finger comes out from a person in this kind of trap, like a branch that extends out, and produces deadly fruit. The trunk of the tree is twisted. This person's case is not hopeless, but the needed help can be blocked by his or her own mask of hypocrisy.

How the person gets to be that way is personal failure, and a mistaken idea of God and of themselves. These can create a need for acceptance by performance. They may beat themselves in the darkness of their closets. But Jesus already took the beating and deep gouges in his back, so they wouldn't have to.

A hypocrite can launch a dangerous weapon. They created the gay lie: they were definitely not innocent in every way, but in an effort to appear so, the women and men attacked those with visible, social blemishes. They threatened and attacked them so much that the victims eventually said, "We're just happy. Nothing to see here. Move on!"

Religious hypocrisy is an abuse that never gets to the root of a problem. It only snips vigorously at the outer leaves. One pain of it is that no performance is ever enough. That is painful! Another pain is that it strikes when people are vulnerable, when they're defenseless, and uncovers people; it does not cover people.

"…love covers a multitude of sins"

But what if God is compassionate, merciful, and bigger than he's often portrayed?

Have you seen Christians very vigorously chopping at same-sex abuse, jumping up and down as on a soap box, impassioned about it with great fervor? But when these same people tolerate what the Bible calls "fornication," in public or in private, it's hypocrisy.

Christians in Western countries are not exempt from the cliffs and ruts common in today's world. But some excuse their own failings while accusing others. This hypocrisy has created a huge rift between religious

Christians and those who wear gay as an identity.

If you look at his own words, the message Jesus brought is really about forgiveness, not about condemning people. It's about mercy—receiving it first from God, and passing it on to all others. That mercy is the foundation of a saved and transformed life.

What if God is so loving that he can minimize mistakes instead of amplifying them? What if he is so merciful and patient and non-judgmental, that he can put anyone at ease, while he operates on them? What if he is so powerful, he's not worried about anyone's current state or past multitude of mistakes? He knows what he can make of each person.

What if he is so free that he can cover a person with his own cloak, made of light, and bring comfort to the weak?

I have pointed out that traditional and religious Christianity is one of the main roots of the gay lie. And yet, I mentioned that the good news, or "gospel"—the central message of the Bible—is liberating and amazing. So what am I?

I started out in the great state of California, an environment that was, unfortunately, characterized by the abuse of sex. As a child, I went through various I mentioned here, and I was greatly led astray as a youth. And Jesus still walked into my life—literally into my room.

When the King came into my life, he did not force me to do anything. He *invited* me. And when I accepted his help, he pulled me up immediately. He introduced me to truth little by little. And as long as I decided to continue forward on his Path, he has always continued to give me Truth. Those Truths gradually adjusted my way of thinking and seeing everything.

Jesus taught me how to use the miracle power of God, as he did while on earth. I am not religious; I'm spiritual. And I believe him 100%. He lifted me when no one else could. And he gave me a new mirror, his Word, to see myself in. It showed me areas where my identity had been covered, and the pathway up. It's a path up a mountain, with challenges and difficulties, but it's the path that leads to glory.

Chapter 10
The Abuse of Sex

Sex is a wonderful servant, but a cruel master.

When you abuse sex, it abuses back. When sexuality is in its place, according to its design, it enhances life. When misused, it is a deep chasm that is difficult to climb out of.

The quality and strength of a society can be measured by its protection for the vulnerable and its teaching and training of youth. The most vulnerable are the children, and the most vulnerable part of a person is their sexuality.

Because of the shame involved, abusing sex creates an area of darkness, of hiding, a "closet"—this is for all abuse of sex, not just some types.

Darkness is an atmosphere. There is a power inside of it. It is the realm of the seducing spirit. The outward picture it uses is something very attractive. But that's just a lure to lead a person off the cliff, into its grip, where it binds and feeds on its victims.

Abusers are mal-programmed. Their brain has been hacked, through what they themselves suffered. They were left with a malfunctioning chip, disorder, and entangled wires. They cry out in agony, in the midst of that control, at times. God loves to help them.

If someone abuses, they don't love you. They love the pleasure center of their brain. They themselves have a deep canyon rut in their thinking that causes them to cycle around to abuse over and over. Both men or women can fall into this trap.

The thing about an abuser is they may seem normal, and then they go into a mode where they become demanding and rough. That's the spirit of abuse, affecting them through the crack in their brain and mind.

The abuse of sex is never victimless. At the least, a person abuses his own brain. Because it's not the actual design of sex, it never actually fulfills. It's like feeding a cookie to a large monster that will surely want more.

Sex was designed to be private, because of its intimate nature. Why do we wear clothes? We are not animals, by any means. For us, clothes are a boundary, for privacy. They're for warmth and for fashion, and they provide a healthy covering. Walls are a boundary. Doors are a boundary. Eyelids are a boundary that can project the eyes if ever need be. Violating privacy is abusive.

A medium, such as a picture or video, can be a loaded weapon that encapsulates and transmits abuse.

People, fundamentally, are *valuable.* A culture that prevents the abuse of sex can easily recognize this. Sexuality is the most inner, intimate part of a person. It is to be kept in maximum security. A jewelry store has the highest security for its highest priced and largest diamonds. And people are the earth's diamonds. But many of us have been lied to, to see ourselves and others as cheap.

For abuse to happen requires a lack of protection. Parents are designed as protectors, but because of widespread deception, ignorance and previous abuses they've suffered, many have laid down their weaponry and left their post. They haven't fulfilled their duties.

When parents provide and protect *physically*, they've only delivered *half* of their responsibility to their children. They also are to teach them and protect their *inner* being, which will determine the outcome of their *whole lives.* In the West, the gatekeepers have been deceived to abandon their post.

A young man should be trained by his father and mother to be a protector for women. This is not to be done primarily by media, nor only by outside role-models *but by parents.* It does "take a village to raise a child," but parents have primary responsibility and influence for this.

Training up a child in this way can be done by words, by example, and by not tolerating abusive messages, in music or other programming. It takes protecting the mind by the Truth, so people don't have to remove society's tampering and brainwashing later.

God gave me a vision once about women, to educate me: they are like the diamonds you see in the window of a high-end jewelry store. The beauty, given to each one of them, is of the most valuable things on earth. They're beauty is on display and can be admired and enjoyed, with protection. But to break the glass from outside, to take one of those diamonds without paying, is illegal. And he'll break his own hand in the process. It's illegal to have them without paying the full price—the covenant commitment to be a companion and protector and true lover and provider, for the rest of one's life.

Sexual pleasure is like a huge, powerful river. Without banks, it results in a flood. On the other hand, strong banks and a strongly built dam, will harness the power of the river for creativity, positive energy, pleasure and fun in many areas of life. And when the right time for the use of sex has come—in the covenant of marriage—there is no disaster.

Ab-use creates fools, who run full speed into a trap. Once in it, they find themselves unable to get out. A trap has bait. A person trained in discretion will be able to see *both* the bait *and* the trap. Something about it is off. It seems "good" but also somehow fake, too good to be true. A wise person hesitates till the deception clears. He or she can then see it as smaller than oneself, understand it, and the trap won't have any power.

The abuse of sex creates shame, but this shame can be wonderfully removed. There is a spiritual wind that will blow it off of one's face powerfully. It will also heal and mend the crack in the thinking and restore a previous boundary.

All can be restored, and light can come that helps a person to never tumble off that cliff, ever again. I'd like to do something for you now, by a supernatural exercise: write down aspects of the abuse of sex you can personally relate to. Just write a list of those things. Then come back. ☺

Now shred the list. Your feelings will change, supernaturally, at that point. And a good remorse will come, for any abuse you've engaged in. This is all supernatural, by the power given to me from above, for you.

Chapter 11

Distorted Relationships

The best and the worst can come through relationships. At their best, light can shine through each person to the other, bringing peace and clarity. At their worst, relationships bring darkness and destruction into your life. The outside may look good, but what comes from the inside can be deadly.

Distorted relationships can be disguised as "for your good," or "because I care about you." But the end of it is poisonous. One person can put a "leash" around another, and use them for their own need, desire, or twisted, sexual pleasure. The relationship can be happily approved by everyone around you, while the person is actually choking you and making you weak.

This kind of abuse is much more than sexual. It's relational. It gets in your head. But you can get out of it, by persistently letting Truth you're your mind to destroy its power.

A distorted relationship is manipulative and crippling. In it, you are defined by the abuser. You are definitely put in a box by them. You can be limited, as on a literal leash of S&M. You're treated as a lower life form, as a pet, trained and under the owner's control—mind-control. You can't get too far without being be yanked back. Everything is good as long as you're limited; the abuser is calm and soothing and caring then, and strokes your ego, as his or her pet.

It is a relationship of control. It is unhealthy. It exists beyond a boundary that the abuser crosses, typically when the victim is going through a vulnerable time.

You have to get literally, far, far away from this kind of person. Any correspondence received should not be given a response. Manipulation and intimidation are the arms of poisonous witchcraft, really, that can stun a person, temporarily paralyzing them.

You need DISTANCE and time to take a breather and begin to get strength. It's like you were suffocated under a pillow—a soft feather pillow that is somehow desirable, but that suffocates! You became disheveled; out of sorts; like a hot mess, trapped in the darkness of seduction.

You can break free! Despite the past, you CAN break free. You'll have to choose a path straight into the desert, so to speak—of temporary isolation that may feel difficult. But if you "the easy way" and stay in the arrangement, the real you will be trapped inside, enclosed and not displayed.

An abuser's philosophy of lies is transferred into the victim's mind over time. It controls the victim from the mind. It also creates a puzzle in the mind. They hold people as under a trance. False guilt is part of the bondage. But a greater power is used to release you from their rope.

IF A WOMAN HAS BEEN TERRIBLY CONSTRICTED and forced, she can develop an insatiable desire to manipulate, dominate and possess. A woman like this will possess or control men; they may possess weaker women who allow them to. They always seem to be in control, always the one with all the cards. Abused men can become this way also.

The strong, controlling grip on the controller can only be pried off with a powerful tool. They can find freedom through forgiving those who terribly abused them.

There is an addiction to emotional-love. That is, control by words and care and kindness, despite the ab-user's ongoing mistreatment of the victim. He or she manipulates a soft spot in a woman's mind and brain, supplying a need for attention, affection, and care—*but not with real love.* Once the abuser worms his or her way into her heart, a dependency is created, so that the victim needs and desires more, which the abuser also keeps "giving." He feeds the victim with bread crumbs continually.

There is healing for you, in the desert. Meaning: first, isolate yourself, far away from the person, or that kind of people, giving them NO ACCESS to you. Second, build your internal defenses by Truth. Get good resources of truth to learn from.[1] Then you will find healing. This is how you have to leave. That one, solid step is the beginning. You've stood up at that point, and you will gain strength to walk forward, through Truth.

So, what does it take to get free from this human web? First, you need an external influence. Someone like me now, reaches through the thick cocoon-like web to find you. You then get room to start to break yourself free and take a breath of fresher air.

Next, step out through the opening in the web that's been made and *escape.* Be very subtle and careful as you do because when the person's radar system is tripped, that person will undoubtedly come to spray your eyes and face, to knock you out again, to fall into their arms. Then they'll put you back into captivity.

Cut the spider-web-like lies with words—words that you speak audibly.

One common lie is that by leaving, you are "hurting" the abuser. You have to say, "I am not hurting that person! Access to me is a privilege, not a right! I *will* live in freedom!!!" Sometimes, the louder you shout it, the better! You're dealing with matters of internal freedom!!!!

Now see yourself accurately. You are *not* a dependent slave! When Africans were put on a slave boat and taken to North and South America, they were *told*, "YOU ARE A SLAVE. You are now the possession of so and so." Those who did not accept that idea or the way things looked, *remained free inside.* They stood with head held high, with dignity. And they fought and found any way to get free. YOU ARE FREE of people, despite the relationship ab-use. Say it of yourself and *act on it.*

Set your sail, alone, and leave your present circumstances. A good wind from the heavens, from God himself, will be at your back, and you will surely arrive at a safe harbor.

[1] For resources, I would recommend Joyce Meyer's teaching, my teaching, and there is other liberating material in today's world

Chapter 12
Death and New LIFE

We've covered several abuses. There is also *self-abuse.* Self-abuse is a tearing at oneself to try to get to a problem and remove it. And it's based on a darkened image of one's own self. It takes place in private. But there is light and cleansing for this also in private, and light to dispel all lies.

There is a solution for all of these things, given by the creator and master-designer. For abuse, he gave a substitute, who would get his hands dirtier than anyone else. He is called, *the Despised and Rejected One.* This is Jesus, who reaches out his nail pierced hands to you now.

He went lower than anyone has ever gone. He bore the wounds and abuse of every person. He had to become acquainted with their pain personally, and their temptations, weakness, grief, sickness, guilt, shame, rejection, curses and all mistakes….

There's a picture of him in the Bible, as of a scapegoat. In ancient Israel they were instructed to take a goat once a year, and the high priest for the nation would put his hands on the goat, to transfer all of the guilt of the whole nation onto that goat. Then he'd release the goat deep into the wilderness. Alone and weighed down with all the people's sins, the goat would eventually collapse, dead. This was a depiction of the one who was coming to remove sins, the Rejected One who would bear all the guilt.

He called himself, "a worm and not a man," when he bore ALL the guilt. He became lower than a man, and eventually his face was "deformed more than that of any man's." This was not just his physical face, but his image before God and man.

He was humiliated, tortured, mocked, spit on, blindfolded and beaten. He was stripped and shown naked to a multitude of people, and he was abandoned by followers, friends and family. This was all done at the hands of evil people. He embraced it, knowing he was a substitute for all of us.

He was called, “the Lamb of God” because he would be sacrificed. So that God could legally remove from us all guilt and error and abuse and shame. Guilt carries shame, and it weighs down on people and can crush their inner being, but there is a Lamb sent from God—Jesus. All of your negative feelings and experiences can be transferred onto his sacrifice, and you walk away totally innocent and free.

Jesus did what no person alive could do: he carried in himself the guilt of every kind and every person as he went to be crucified. He was tortured and died as a convict. But *really*, he had done nothing wrong.

He was not executed for his own crimes or internal sins or goings astray. It was for yours and mine. It was so our slate can be completely erased, and God can clothe us in his own right-ness—*for no more guilt.*

This is a totally undeserved gift. When Jesus was sacrificed, by God’s will and his own will, it was a true, love gift, to all of humanity.

Imagine, all wrongs ever done by human hands, compensated for in a single sacrifice. Imagine the consequences removed too, and the internal wound from abuse healed, so that it dries up and has no more leakage.

The sacrifice-event, accomplished once for all time, created the greatest covering, and God will clothe you with it. You no longer need to cover yourself up because of feeling shame.

Jesus was raised from the dead, three days after his crucifixion, and was made the Lord of all by the Father. He is “the Lord” which means the highest authority of all. And he is the King, in what’s called, the Kingdom of God and of Light. That Kingdom is near you now, to free and save you completely from every abusive desire that would otherwise hold you.

To receive God’s love-gift of total forgiveness and peace with God, you need to call on Jesus as the Lord that he is, and ask him to save you. No matter what you have done, he will then forgive and cover you—no doubt, no question.

Jesus broke out of the prison of death, forever, and now he saves people. This is not a religious thing. You're not joining a religion; you are being freed.

If you call on him, recognizing his high place now and yielding completely to him, he will save you now. You are acknowledging the greatest and eternal King—who became the Lamb and already died for every error of humanity out of love. Do so now, and he will free you. Then come back to this book.

Jesus drank liquid death all the way down. He didn't stop till he tasted death for every human. What is death? It's not just when the spirit leaves the body—that's only physical death. Death is characterized by limitation and restriction. Imagine a coffin. Someone is in there and can't move; they're stuck in that box. That's what death looks like. Jesus took it, so that all people—no matter how much abuse they've committed or suffered—can experience transformation and resurrected Life.

Jesus' death became the death of your old nature, if you called on him. He did this to give you a new and indestructible Life, to change your actual identity and give you a new nature—one with him. When he rose, you also rose so that you now have a new life that is indestructible.

Alive in this new life, you have a new nature. You have been fused together with the Son of God, and when you rose with him you experienced a new birth, on the inside. You were re-born, of God. You are now, like him, divine-royalty, a Child of God.

Your nature changed when you were born of God. You swapped out the old one, passed down from our first human ancestors. It was equally defective in all humans, but that did not make us less valuable or less loved. God our creator still loved us, and he sent rescue from above. He watched as Jesus was crucified, but it was not only Jesus, but also the defective nature of humanity, through him.

The new, resurrected life has no error. You bear the nature of God. You are part of his Family now. You escaped the world system, also consequences from past abuses and failures of any kind.

This new nature makes up a new identity for you. It marks a new start, the beginning of a new race you are running in life, with a glorious end. You're now a part of what is called the "New Man," being joined with

Jesus in his resurrection from the dead. And your sins/errors/mistakes in life were ALL forgiven through him.

Now acknowledge it out loud. Say, "Jesus is my Lord, my Savior, my King. I have new life now in him. And I was forgiven and pardoned by him, completely. I am a new-born Child of God now. My new life has begun."

Physically speaking now, if you are trapped in prostitution, it's time to fly away. Ask God for an opening, a way out. You will see through it to the outside. Make sure to take that way out *immediately*, even not knowing what's out there for you. God will guide you and provide for you, ***as you go***. For freedom, this is not optional.

If you are currently in a relationship that involves the ab-use of sexuality with a person or images, whether opposite or same-sex, leave the situation and start again. Talk to Jesus and your Father, God, about everything, and make fast moves to *get out of there.*

Chapter 13
So What is It Really?

You have come out of the grave with Jesus into new Life. You can begin to see now what's really going on, down on earth. I said about "the gay lie," that it is a shield, a defense against accusation and discrimination. It seems like a warm, safe place, but it's actually a trap.

The Bible speaks of creation, how God made the first man unisex, neither male nor female. This reveals why *sexuality* is not defining. You are not your sex—even male and female. Though your body is on or the other, *you* are higher than that. God breathed into the first man "the breath [or "spirit"] of lives" (literal Hebrew): that is, Adam and Eve.

Later, he separated Eve out from man, and there was now wo-man, male and female. The attraction of male and female started here, as they had been one to begin with. Their re-union was the first marriage—a life-long, committed relationship.

This unique relationship had the power to produce offspring. The male and female fit together in every way, including sexually, and they had God's blessing within that covenant. After bringing the two together, he called everything "very good."

The covenant-commitment is a union. In today's modern world, there's a marriage certificate that goes with this and usually a wedding. But it was the sincere, full commitment of this male and female that was the real union. Then when they came together sexually, God "tied them together." This is what the Bible describes.

It also speaks against casual divorce, for the sake of the children and because God actually "tied the two together." So, there's the mutual decision to marry, and then there's the spiritual bonding that God himself does at the time of joining sexually. Jesus said about this, "Man should not separate what God [supernaturally] tied together."

The relationship is designed to give the children the complete picture of God as they grow up because original "Man" was made according to God's image, which includes a combination of both male and female.

So a unified male and female cooperating in raising the kids with love, protection, instruction, and training gives the kids a picture of God. It gives them security and nourishment, a balanced blend of the two opposite sexes, like the sun and the moon. It also gives them a picture of resilience and working through differences, which they can use in their own future marriage. This causes the fabric of society to stay intact.

These things were God's design. Every other use of private parts, other than to pee, is outside of the boundaries of God's original design and intent. That said, whenever anyone ever engaged in *any* of those things, God has never put that person in a different category of being nor give them a new identity. Humans did that.

The abnormal use of sexuality never put anyone in a separate category from anyone else. It's an action, not an identity. It didn't redefine them nor did it reclassify them. It never initiated mockery from God, nor from any of the People of God representing him accurately. Never.

Whenever the Bible describes someone who is or has engaged in homosexuality, it simply refers to the person as a "man" or "woman." 'Never anything beyond that. You were not different than anyone else.

Does it affect the person significantly on the inside. Yes, of course it does, because the design of sexuality and its strong impact on the brain. That's why there were boundaries put in place, to protect people.

Jesus is referred to as the perfect representation of God (not the Law of Moses, which only had power to condemn and not to save). It was he who showed God's true nature and ways. As King, he is also the Judge, in God's Kingdom. How did Jesus respond to the various alterations of God's original design of sexuality? Always, it was with compassion and healing.

Jesus minimized sexual errors. He called them sicknesses, identified himself as the Doctor and proceeded to heal them. He had the scalpel and skill needed that could show a person their true identity, while separating out from within them whatever was hurting them and others.

The staunchly religious people of Jesus' day didn't like his compassionate and healing approach, and they labeled him a "friend of sinners." Many of his early followers had been involved in sexual error.

Oxford Dictionary calls "perversion": "the alteration of something from its original course, meaning, or state to a distortion of…what was first intended." Among Jesus' followers in the Bible, some had been involved in sexual alterations, including same-sex related, *and others.* This is stated openly in the Bible.

I want to point out the alterations of God's design for sex mentioned in the Bible. Again, it's important to see these as completely separate from identity, and to know that God's view is compassion. His power is totally available for healing and realignment today!!!

1. Adultery—sexual union with someone else's spouse
2. Covetousness—desiring someone else's spouse for oneself
3. Fornication—from the Greek word, "pornea": engaging in sex without lifetime commitment; can be for money or not
4. Impurity/uncleanness—this refers to actions that "defile" or make dirty, from the outside. That mud can be washed off, no matter how thick. These actions are not actual, sexual intercourse, and can include:
    - Ek-pornea—literally, "out of fornication" (remember this one because we'll come back to it)
    - Imagining fornication, adultery or other perversions. The modern "porn industry" and entertainment that pushes the boundaries (typically for money) is in this category
    - "Masturbation"—literally, "hand-defilement"). This was largly unknown in the old world; it began with sexualized media images, and is not the normal use of the sex organs, which were designed for bonding in a covenant-relationship
    - Child-abuse/molestation—a serious and terrible violation of boundaries. A child's body hasn't developed, and they are to be protected, never abused
    - Anything else outside of natural and spiritual boundaries, e.g., "lying with an animal," a plant, a rock, [fill in the blank]…

These four categories are all alterations of God's original design and can be part of another Greek, Bible word: "unrestraint." Translations use many rarely known words such as "licentiousness," "lasciviousness," "wantonness," "sensuality," "insolence," or "incontinence" for this word. They all really just mean "sexual unrestraint" or "going beyond the boundaries."

Now consider the fourth category, "uncleanness." I listed several variations of it. Though widely different from each other, each is an alteration from what God designed and gave. Where is homosexuality on this list? It is referred to as, "ek-pornea" in the Bible, literally, *"out of fornication."*

Homosexuality emerges out of fornication because once the river of sexuality crosses its banks, it will continue to expand into various other areas. Also fornication brings shame, and that overflows with accusations, which falls on those with any appearance of same-sex attraction. The accusation backs innocent people up into a corner where they have to defend themselves.

Homosexuality is, for many, outside of people's personal choosing. It truly often starts with abuse. But what I'd like to point out is that it is just another alteration. It is in the same category as masturbation.

All ab-use of sexuality hurts the brain. It's all called in the Bible, "a sin against one's own body" and creates, "a penalty within oneself" for that reason. In other words, an unintended, distorted desire follows it, just because of the strong connection between sexuality and the pleasure center of the brain. But though easily damageable, it is healable also. There is Truth that enlightens and sets free. We can *supernaturally*, "be transformed by the renewing of the mind." These are all provisions from above.

Back to understanding the brain. The change that takes place in the brain results in something else in the Bible called, "excessive desire." In the original language it is "epi-thymia," literally, "over-desire" or "a desire beyond natural desire." Don't feel bad because this can be reduced and disappear too!

In the original language, this strong or excessive desire, can be good or bad depending on what it's for. If bad, it can be based on past experiences that have opened up mental pathways and altered sensitive desires of the brain. It's typically translated "lust" or "longing." though it's typically not sexual, in the Bible.

"Excessive desire" is not actually an error/sin in the Scripture (see, for example, James 1:14-15 in the Bible), and it can come from different sources. It is just characteristic of the current state of our physical, moldable, pleasure center of the brain. No matter where anyone is at, they can breathe a big sigh of relief at this point, and smile.

A distortion of desires and feelings *is not you.* We should never own or feel bad about those but recognize and "deny" them when they show up, based on Truth we're learning (see, for example, Titus 2:12 in the Bible). We verbally reject them and dig a new mental pathway for ourselves. It can be hard work, but it's well worth it. As we put a stop to those desires, in view of the Truth about our new identity, and other Truths, they gradually change. Don't be intimidated by them or backed into a corner.

Temptation is also *not you.* Temptation is from the outside, and is not wrong. The Bible reveals clearly that while on earth Jesus was tempted in every way any human could ever be. This would include *every* perversion of sexuality listed above, and many other things. This is why He is so FULL of compassion for you. Everything anyone has ever been tempted by, he was tempted by.

So was Jesus tempted to cross boundaries and to allow others to cross his boundaries? Yes. He was a man, with flesh and blood. But he didn't give in to these temptations. Though scratched from the outside, he remained unscarred.

Why was Jesus tempted so much, more than any other person? To overcome all temptation, as a man, to learn compassion, and to have power to deal with all issues! He has power to rewire the pleasure center of anyone's brain. He will help you with it. He has special compassion toward all who are tempted in any way, and he will help. Just talk to him about it.

So what is "homosexuality"? *First* of all, it is not an identity. It is not a new category of people, but an activity and mental desire.

Secondly, it's not a root but a symptom. Roots are the ideas we swallow, our tragic experiences, our way of being raised, and our way of being treated by those around us.

Thirdly, it's not an "inexcusable offense," but something God has deep compassion on and lovingly heals, just as he does with fornication or adultery or unclean thoughts or masturbation…

Fourthly, if you can handle the truth spoken in love, I will tell you this also: it is not actually sex. Sexual union requires the two opposites sex organs. Anything that doesn't include the male and female sex organs is actually not sex, but in the category of uncleanness, with other ab-uses such as masturbation.

Although it is outside of God's intent and boundaries, it does *not* involve two people being tied together by God into "one flesh," so it is not on the level of fornication or adultery. And these two are healable also.

Fifthly, it is related to confusion. Why? God created the covenant relationship of male and female with distinctive roles. A same-sex relationship is like the original, with one person acting as if they are the opposite sex, when they're not. They can truly start to think of themself as the opposite sex, but that's actually confusion.

This confusion can be a mesmerizing influence of domination, by the stronger partner. It can *definitely* be temporary. By getting fully away from the dominating person you remove yourself from the influence. Then you'll need to not allow anyone else of the same sex from taking that place in your life, no matter how much they may try. (Overly strong people can sense when someone is still healing and not very strong yet).

In the Bible, same-sex alteration is always listed alongside other alterations and errors. There is no separate category for it!! And the Great Doctor, Jesus, and people like myself, have special compassion on it. And we can heal it by the power of God!

You are a son or daughter *of God*. You passed from darkness to Light, and it had nothing to do with sexuality. It had to do with Jesus. If you are his now, let the glorious, Loving One define you with his Words. Sit quietly now, before him, and ask him to.

Now write down whatever he shared with you. What he says about you is true, glorious, and a solid foundation you can build your life on.

Chapter 14
Consequences and Healing

Rape does not just affect the body, but the mind. All sexual ab-uses do.

As compassionate as God is, as patient and tolerant and forgiving as he is, once an individual or society knows what his original design of sex is, he requires them to start to change to it.

For example, God warns against fornication. In the Bible he says, "run away from it." Why? Because it scars the mind. That is a built-in consequence, but God also judges people who know better and still abuse others sexually. This is not man's judgmental-ness, but God's anger can be kindled, like a fire, and eventually burn hot because he's a God of love and justice.

For example, when children are abused and cry out to their creator, he steps in and intervenes. Abusive parents have suffered early deaths or incarcerations this way. A final judgment day is also coming. People should know that what we do in our lives has real consequences.

As much as Jesus forgave sins, he also lovingly and caringly told people to change their lifestyle. "I don't condemn you. Now go and don't sin in this way anymore," he said in one case. That is the complete picture. He forgave and freed one man powerfully and said, "stop sinning so nothing worse happens to you." There are spiritual forces, there are venereal diseases, and there are mental consequences that are very real, and God doesn't want them to reach us.

Jesus also said, "Whoever sins is a slave to sin." Sin has power to enslave. He also spoke of how he will free people, through his sacrifice and through the truth they receive.

The good news is that wrong mental pathways can be filled in.

God's acceptance is real, and he needs time to work on us and fulfill us, in a new lifestyle, to "straighten us out." This is *all* out of love and his goodness toward us.

Jesus compared evil spirits to flies that hang out around defilement. But by continually receiving the Words of God, the Spirit of God will blow them away, clearing one's whole atmosphere!

It is God's Words that cleanses and heals our thinking and polishes us, to show our true identity. As you continue to receive them, eventually you will overflow with life-giving truth for others. They will long to receive just one drop of God's Word from you.

Chapter 15
Strength for Stability

The societies we live in today, especially in the Western world, have a lot of seduction. The goal of seduction is to silence you, captivate you, and pull you back to where you were before. The truths in this chapter will teach you how to prevent that. I will share with you what I call, "first steps in God's Kingdom."

God is a great King, and when you acknowledge Jesus as your Lord, you've entered into his domain. It's called, The Kingdom of Light, and that light expels all darkness and blindness.

God's Kingdom is a place of maximum security, for you. It's a place of child-like innocence, freedom and joy. Here, God your Father prepares spiritual food for you, to nourish you for your journey on his path. You have a covering here, by the sacrifice of the Anointed King, Jesus.

The **first step** after hearing the real message about Jesus is to call on him to save you, as your Lord. This is leaving behind your old life, regardless of what background you're from, and starting a new one, within his boundaries, and with a new, clear identity.

Your next and **second step** is to be immersed in water. This has traditionally been called "baptism." All it really means is to be immersed in water, in Jesus' royal Authority (or "Name"). It is not a religious ritual, *and you don't need a traditional building or "priest" or ceremony to do it!* It's a power-act, with cleansing power. It is a part of your personal pledge to God.

Anyone can immerse you anywhere. As long as you are sincere with Jesus, it will be extremely powerful. Those who are serious will always go through with this. You can do it, today, wherever you are. You can use a bathtub, a pool, a river.... There is no ritual to it. Just know it's in Jesus's

Name, who you recognized as the risen Lord of all.

Along with that, the Lord Jesus will give you a Spirit-immersion—your **step three**. He immerses you with God's own Spirit and with spiritual fire. This is an instant, transformative experience, a gift that empowers and enlightens you. If you read the Book of Acts in the Bible, you will see this gift received over and over by God's People.[2]

Your **fourth step** is the discovery of all God made you to be, by your new birth. He will show you "the new you" as you receive His Word. His Word is found in the Bible, and in His set apart People, who know how to speak the Truth in Love. You'll know them because they have *life* on the inside of them and speak truth in love. They're not perfect but sincere and growing.

Step five is worship—your response to God—and the Word you receive for transformation. Receiving God's word is how you grow spiritually. The book of Psalms says, "The entrance of your Words brings light" because *when God, your Father, speaks to you, light comes into your heart with it.* To have this, you have to make room in your heart for him to speak. He speaks when we listen, when we open our heart to new information and his perspective, which is new to us. Over time, you learn to let him lead you into the Truth. Every time he leads you into any truth, you step into new freedom in that area. Our freedom is found in the Light that comes in with his Word.

So as you read the Bible, for example the books of Mark, John, James, Hebrews, etc., do so while also listening to Him. Talk to him first. Ask him to share something with you before you read. Then be attentive for that; you'll become a skilled expert in hearing him very quickly! This is how to receive Light through his Words. Don't worry about what you don't understand; those details will become clear over time. What's important is that you connect with Him and with His Truth, while receiving his Words.

As you listen, you grow. As you put into practice what you receive from him, your foundation hardens. You become established in God's Truth. As you think of the Truth that you've made room for in your heart, it becomes a shield for you from outside, intrusive forces. As you *speak*

---

[2] If you have questions about this, I wrote about it extensively in a booklet, "Our Supernatural Help," which is also Chapter 26 of my book, "For Freedom."

God's Truth that you receive (whether alone or to others), there is also a spiritual fire that comes out of your mouth. It repels any evil influence around you. They are completely vulnerable to God's word spoken out of your mouth.

Step six is relationship with God's People. You were re-born into a community of God's living People, who stand and have fire in their eyes.

Eventually, you will come across leadership. If they are spiritually mature, you will be able to receive from them, and they will be able to help you skillfully. Respect them, listen to and learn from them, but always keep your main focus on the Lord Jesus and God your Father. There is no distance between you and them, and no one between you and them.

There are also sincere, growing, spiritual communities. These three: the Word of God in various forms, good leadership, and a sincere, loving and growing community are what you need to start a spiritual "bonfire."

As you grow *together* alongside a community, you'll learn to be *interdependent.* Not completely dependent (or "codependent") on anyone, and not independent or isolated from other true Believers, which isn't healthy. Instead, you'll learn to give and receive, in community, and be at peace with yourself and others. This is God's gift to you.

At first, you may face the monster called, "rejection." It is not you, but it communicates ideas to you, like "you are different than everyone else, not worthy to be a part of the pack," etc.—all lies. Simply speak words like, "I am accepted by God, and those who know God will recognize me." You can beat the spirit of rejection through God and Truth, and by not isolating, even when you really want to.

You don't go back in time to "start over." Much better: you were transported to a different place spiritually, so that now all things are actually new for you. And the glory of the light of your new location will also sort out your sexuality. It can do so *easily*.

God will give you his original intent for sexuality and way better than "normal" or average. He will give you the true, to replace the counterfeit, and you will always have a supernatural dimension to your life as you grow.

Married sex was designed to be the beginning of all sexuality. He will heal your mind and give *that* to you. There are a very few who he actually calls to not marry, either for a season or even longer term. It's rare and definitely not his norm, and you don't have to try to volunteer yourself into that slim category.[3] Also don't worry about feelings; *they will come eventually*, like the dawn of a clear, new day.

When you came into Jesus the King, God actually made you a virgin. You were not only forgiven, but you were made new supernaturally. And any disease in your blood dries up now also. If it's on your skin, it is right now removed so that you are healed.

Don't worry about your past or background. God has always had people with a variety of backgrounds, including those who practiced a spectrum of different sexual lifestyles—*always*. All come through Jesus into Newness of Life, as brand new (see 1Corinthians Chapter 6, verses 9-11 and 2Corinthians Chapter 5, verse 17, in the Bible).

Live a continual life of forgiveness and mercy/compassion. We who have been embraced by Jesus, with so much love, can *never* look down on *anyone*. We can never point a finger at anyone. We turn and embrace whoever allows us to, like he did us.

Know that images have *power*. Look at and indulge in the images that bring Light into your being. To do anything, people need an image. An image is a form to build into, like concrete needs a form to fill and harden in. God has images for you, in his Word and in his People, including via media, that you can see and fill into. Utilizing God-inspired images will cause you to advance on the path he has for you.

Images are seeds, of Life or restriction. Images come through words or directly as pictures. Both caution and confidence are the guardrails that protect us from dangerous ones. Carefulness keeps you from unnecessary, wrong, "trip-line" images, at the wrong time. Confidence allows you to bat them down when you do see them, so that they don't stick to your mind and hurt you. You know you're bigger than them, so you're bold, while also cautious.

God-inspired images are fun and empowering! They're not just

---

[3] Jesus called those people "eunuchs for the Kingdom of God" and called it a supernatural gift (see Matthew Chapter 19, verse 12, in the Bible)

interesting. You can enjoy them with the innocence of a child. God wants this for you *in place* of the other. It's a new lifestyle with exposure to new things. It's not enough to just abstain; we have to replace.

You'll discover promises of God in his Word. As you look into your future, through them, you will see amazing, beautiful, and glorious things. His Spirit will show you those *good* things that are to come, *in your life*. See them from afar, smile at them, indulge in those light-filled, good pictures (or "visions") about your future life. And they *will* become a realty, whether sooner or later. No matter what happens, never let go of those images.

Your WHOLE LIFE will fit into the new molds of the images God will show you. They will be a royal crown of glory on your head, around your thinking. You will think only on the level of His Kingdom and glory and honor. And as a reward for doing so, you will share his reign, both now and forever and ever and ever—your glory with him will never end.

Persevere in these things. You will get tired at times. You're running a race! But as you continue in this way meticulously, you will always receive a spiritual boost by the Spirit of God. You will find and enjoy his strength, in place of your own.

About The Author

By God's favor, David O'Brien is a joyful husband and a father of two daughters, an author, public speaker, facilitator, and Life coach.

David is the author of the book and song, "For Freedom," and producer of the Royal-Freedom Podcast. He also founded The Kingdom Courses and Lights in the World.

David serves as an intl. director within Christ Love Ministries Intl., and co-leader at the Kingdom Embassy Intl HQ, founded by Ap Charles and Pst Donna Ndifon, in RI, USA. David and his wife, Sonia, founded East-West Services, a 501c3, to prevent and alleviate human trafficking and bullying, especially among youth.

David spent years living and serving abroad in several countries of Africa and Asia and has written several books, including "For Freedom," "Heal the Sick," "In Search of The Bride," "Return to Acts Christianity," and "SHINE (Daughter of God, It Is Your Time)." David champions freedom and distinctiveness in the world, through the Living Word of the Anointed King.

For more information or to request David to speak in your venue, visit

www.Royal-Freedom.com

More Help from Above

Free gift-resource available at **www.Royal-Freedom.com**

Podcasts on Spotify (free & paid episodes)

- Royal-Freedom Podcast, by David O'Brien
- Lovely Talk for Lovely Women, by Sonia O'Brien

Books by David O'Brien

- The New Creation in Male and Female
- For Freedom
- A Pure Path
- In Search of the Bride: The King is Looking for The One

Books by Other Authors

- An Affair of the Mind, by Laurie Hall
- Love Hunger, by David Kyle Foster
- Truth Behind the Fantasy of Porn, by Shelley Lubben

Mini-Courses, on Demand by David O'Brien

- Kept for His Purpose
- The Power of a Single Eye, Parts 1, 2 & 3
- That The World May Know
- The Path of Purity

Kingdom Courses by David O'Brien – TheKingdomCourses.com
Introductory: First Steps in The Kingdom

1. Reigning on The Kingdom Foundation
2. For Freedom in The King
3. Salvations of the King
4. Be Strong in the Lord
5. The King's Legislature

Royal-Freedom Mentorship (1 on 1 or group) – Royal-Freedom.com

Empower Media Network

- www.EmpowerMediaNetwork.com
- Also on YouTube, Instagram, Facebook & X

RECOMMEND THIS BOOK – If you found this book to be enlightening, and you'd like to share how it has helped you, feel free to share your story with us via info@thebondagebreaker.com. Include your name and location, and a photo or video if you can. Thank you!

BUY IN BULK – You can buy copies of this book in bulk for distribution via our website, **www.Royal-Freedom.com**.

I invite you to take my course, *"First Steps in The Kingdom"* here. It covers 10 first steps including how to read the Bible:

www.ingramcontent.com/pod-product-compliance
Lightning Source LLC
LaVergne TN
LVHW011051110826
845149LV00015B/3447

* 9 7 8 1 9 6 0 2 4 5 1 6 8 *